Other titles in the series:

David Beckham

978 0 7496 8232 3

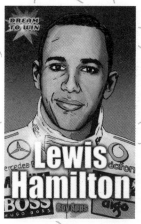

Lewis Hamilton

978 0 7496 8233 0

Hope Powell

978 0 7496 8235 4

For Tom Apps, the straightest bat around

First published in 2008 by
Franklin Watts
338 Euston Road
London NW1 3BH

Franklin Watts Australia
Level 17/207 Kent Street
Sydney NSW 2000

Text © Roy Apps 2008
Illustrations © Chris King 2008
Cover design by Peter Scoulding

A CIP catalogue record for this book
is available from the British Library.

ISBN: 978 0 7496 8234 7

Dewey Classification: 796.358'092

1 3 5 7 9 10 8 6 4 2

Printed in Great Britain

Franklin Watts is a division of Hachette Children's Books,
an Hachette Livre UK company.
www.hachettelivre.co.uk

Note from the Author:

Everyone knows Monty Panesar as 'Monty'; so Monty is what we've called
him in this book. His full name is Mudhsuden Singh Panesar.

Monty Panesar

Roy Apps

Illustrated by Chris King

FRANKLIN WATTS
LONDON•SYDNEY

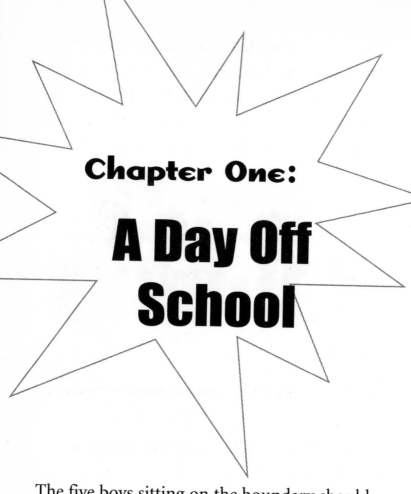

Chapter One:

A Day Off School

The five boys sitting on the boundary should all have been at school. Instead, they had come to watch a cricket match. Sachin Tendulkar, the greatest batsman in the world, and their number one hero, was playing for the touring Indian side against the local county, Northamptonshire.

The boys cheered his every stroke. When he reached his 50, Tendulkar turned, smiled and waved his bat at them. In reply, the boys started to sing and dance wildly. The small cricket ground at Luton, a small town in England, had seen nothing like it before.

After the match, the tallest of the boys opened his kit bag and took out his cricket bat. "I'm going to get Sachin Tendulkar to sign this," he announced. He had a dream of becoming a great batsman like Tendulkar. "Well, I don't suppose any of us will ever see him again."

He wasn't to know it; but he was wrong, very wrong indeed.

The club where the five friends played cricket was the Luton Indians Cricket Club Juniors. It was only a small club, but their coach Hitu Naik was a passionate and dedicated man. One day he heard that the county cricket club were holding Junior trials.

"Does anybody fancy having a go?" he asked.

A lot of the younger boys put their hands up, but some of the older ones looked unsure.

"That sort of thing is for boys from posh, private schools," said one of them. "They've all got better equipment and training grounds than we have. They'll be much better than us."

"That is a very bad attitude," replied Hitu Naik, sternly. "You all have dreams, don't you, of playing cricket at the highest level?"

They nodded.

"Well, none of you are going to achieve those dreams unless you always aim to test yourself against the very best. The county trials are a golden opportunity to do just that. Now, I'll ask again, who would like to go in for them?"

This time, everyone put their hands up, including the boy who'd had his bat signed by Sachin Tendulkar. His name was Monty Panesar.

Chapter Two:

The Trials

The trials took place at a smart, private school in Bedford. As Monty and his friends piled out of the back of Hitu Naik's old van, they saw that the car park was full of gleaming new cars.

The trials were hard. All the other boys had been coached at their schools by highly qualified and highly paid professionals. They all wore the latest cricket gear, including proper helmets. Monty just tried to thump as many balls as hard as he could, the way he had seen the great Sachin Tendulkar do.

On the way home in Hitu Naik's van, the boys were in a bad mood.

"The rest of them were so good," one of the boys sighed. "And so smart."

"Don't worry," said Hitu Naik. "You did your best and you've had the chance to play with the top young players in the county."

Everyone still looked glum.

"Come on! Cheer up," said Hitu Naik. "The day you stop enjoying your cricket is the day you should stop playing. Let's see some smiles."

One by one the boys began to smile. The smiles turned to laughter and soon everyone was joking about the day's events: the balls they had bowled, the shots they had played and the cars they had seen.

Chapter Three:

A Promise

At the next practice night, the boys were still talking about the county trials.

"Can we go again next year?" one of the younger boys asked Hitu Naik.

"Some of you can, but not all of you."

There was a murmur of disappointment. "Why not?" everyone chorused.

"Because," Hitu Naik went on, "I had a call from the county youth coach earlier this evening." He paused. "Five of you have been chosen for the county youth teams!"

A gasp ran around the room, followed by absolute silence as Hitu Naik read out the names. The last name to be called out was… Monty Panesar.

After all the congratulations were over, Hitu Naik took Monty and the other four boys to one side.

"There's something else you should know," he said. "I was having a few drinks with another coach in the bar. This other coach wasn't very complimentary about our set up here."

Monty looked around at the ramshackle clubhouse and thought back to the smart surroundings of the school in Bedford. He could understand what that coach had meant.

"That made me so angry," Hitu Naik said. "We may not have professional coaches or be able to afford the best equipment, but we work very hard and you boys are all talented. So I told this other coach… I said 'one day that smirk will be wiped from your face!'

"And he said 'Oh yes? When?'"

"And I replied, 'When I come into this bar and tell you that one of my lads is playing cricket for England.'"

The boys stared at him in silence and disbelief. Hitu Naik looked at them all. "Do you know what this ignorant coach did? He laughed. Laughed! So, I don't care which one of you it is," he said. "But I have to prove this coach wrong. Promise you won't let me down?"

"We promise!" chorused the boys. And from that moment Monty had just one dream: to play cricket for England.

Chapter Four:

End of the Dream?

Every time he batted for the county youth team, Monty tried hard to play better strokes. Each day of the week he practised, just as Hitu Naik had taught him. He even went down to the park in the winter snow.

But deep down, Monty knew that his dream of being an England batsman was just not going to come true. His batting was good, but it was not getting any better. The trouble was, the county saw him as a fast bowler and each week when the fixture lists went up, he found himself batting at number 10 or 11. Some weeks he didn't get to bat at all. Besides, he was gangly and flat-footed, not a natural, graceful athlete at all. He knew they didn't see him as a top-class batsman, let alone a future England player.

One day a new bowling coach arrived at the county ground. He watched Monty bowl.

"OK!" he said after Monty had bowled a few fast balls in the nets, "I've seen enough. You can take a break now."

Monty slouched off. He could tell by the coach's tone that he didn't rate his bowling one bit. His dream of one day becoming a good enough cricketer to play for England seemed even further away.

To stop himself getting too downhearted, Monty started playing around with a spare cricket ball. He tried a few spinners, enjoying seeing the ball curve through the air and take off in different directions as it thudded into the pitch. He turned around and saw the coach a few metres away, watching him.

"Let's take a look at your hands, lad," said the coach.

Puzzled, Monty held out his hands. They were large – very large – and his fingers were strong and long.

"I thought so! They're not a fast bowler's hands," said the coach.

"Oh," said Monty, sadly. He turned away to hide his disappointment, certain now that his dream of playing for England was well and truly over.

"No," the coach went on, "you've got perfect spinner's hands. Large and strong – just right for gripping the ball."

"Really?" said an amazed Monty. "Are you sure?"

"Of course I'm sure! I should know. I was a spinner myself once."

"Who for?" asked Monty.

"Northamptonshire and England," replied
the coach.

Back at the Luton Indians Club, Monty told
Hitu Naik what the county coach had said:
"Me? A spinner? My dream is to be a
batsman and a fast bowler for England."

"If a man who's been an England spinner says
you have the makings of a spinner, then
you've got to listen to him," said Hitu Naik.

Chapter Five:

Practice, Practice, Practice!

So Monty started to learn a new skill: the art and craft of spin bowling. He practised with his brother, he practised with his mates and he practised with Hitu Naik. If there was no one around, he simply dropped a handkerchief on the ground, walked the length of a cricket pitch, then bowled and tried to hit the handkerchief again and again and again.

After one match for Bedfordshire, Monty was approached by a man who had been watching him for the whole game. "I'm from Northamptonshire County Cricket club," he said. "Would you like to come up to the County ground for a trial?"

Monty didn't need to be asked twice. 'Northants' were a first-class county, who had international players among their top eleven players.

After his trial, Monty was invited into the Chief Executive's office.

"Have you ever considered becoming a professional cricketer?" the Chief Executive asked him.

"Oh yes," replied Monty. "My ambition is to play for England."

The Chief Executive raised an eyebrow. Monty blushed, worried that his dream made him sound big-headed.

"In the meantime," the Chief Executive said, "how would you like to join us as a professional, for the summer?"

Hitu Naik was thrilled to hear the news. "Don't forget Monty," he said, "I've got to prove that snobby coach in the bar wrong and get one of my juniors into the England team. At the moment, you look the man most likely to do it."

It didn't seem that way to Monty. Although he was a professional cricketer now, he had yet to play for the Northamptonshire first team. Not only that, but he was still part-time: the rest of the year he was a Computer Engineering student.

He knew there was only one way to succeed; the way that Hitu Naik had taught him: play as much as possible and practice, practice, practice.

Gradually over the years, Monty established himself in the Northamptonshire first team. One day, in 2005, he took 10 wickets in a match against Yorkshire. His captain congratulated him.

"That was brilliant," he said. "And better still, one of the England selectors was in the crowd. He's helping to choose the Academy squad. You're bound to be named!"

Monty's heart leapt. Being in the England Academy squad was the first step to becoming an England player.

So when the squad for the Academy was published, Monty studied it eagerly. But however hard he looked, his name wasn't on the list.

His hopes of playing for England had been dashed yet again.

Chapter Six:

A Surprise Phone Call

Keep playing, that's what Monty knew he had to do, and that is what he wanted to do. He spent the winter in Australia playing grade cricket.

When he came back to England in the spring he got a phone call from the selectors.

They wanted him to go to Loughborough so they could see how he was progressing. Perhaps, Monty thought excitedly, they wanted him to join the Academy squad, after all?

One morning, Monty was playing touch rugby as part of a warm-up session, when the Academy coach called him across. Could this be the moment he had been waiting for? Was the coach going to ask him to join the Academy squad?

"Call for you, Monty," the coach said, holding out his mobile phone.

Monty's face couldn't hide his disappointment, but the coach had a broad grin on his face.

"Who is it?" asked Monty, puzzled.

"Oh, didn't I say? It's David Graveney. Chairman of the England selectors. He wants a word with you."

"The Chairman of the England selectors? You mean –"

"Are you going to speak to him, or not?" asked the coach, still grinning.

Monty took the coach's mobile. "Hello?"

"Monty? David Graveney here. Congratulations. You've been picked for the England squad to go to India."

Monty's heart was racing. The England squad? He was about to say sorry, there must be some mistake. I haven't played a full season as a professional yet! Luckily, he stopped himself just in time.

He still couldn't believe it when he rang his parents and told them the news; nor when he phoned Hitu Naik. His old coach was over the moon, though. "I can go and see that snobby coach I met in the bar and say 'one of my lads is playing for England'," he laughed. "That will wipe the smirk off his face!"

"I'm only in the squad. I've not been picked for the team, yet," said Monty.

"You will!" said Hitu Naik. He laughed again. "And then you'll have to work hard. You know who you'll have to bowl to, don't you?"

Only then did Monty realise. "Sachin Tendulkar!" he gulped. The greatest batsman in the world and his boyhood hero.

Chapter Seven:

Howzat!

The first Test Match was at Nagpur, India. It was the first time Monty and ever been to a Test Match, let alone played in one. When he came on to bowl for the first time all he could think was 'thank goodness it's not Tendulkar who's batting.'

The next day England's fast bowlers got to work. In the space of two overs, three wickets fell. There was a frenzied cheer from the 35,000 spectators as Sachin Tendulkar – their hero and Monty's hero – strode out to the wicket. A few overs later, Andrew Flintoff, the England captain, tossed the ball to Monty.

Suddenly, Monty was nervous. He had to concentrate; try to imagine that Tendulkar was just another, ordinary batsman.
Tendulkar, the greatest batsman in the world, his hero!

Monty bowled again and again; and again and again Tendulkar prodded the ball forward, defensively. Then, suddenly, as if from nowhere, Monty bowled a ball that straightened up just enough to miss the bat and thump Tendulkar on his pad.

"Y-e-e-e-e-s-s-s-s!!!!!" yelled Monty.

"Howzat!!!" roared the rest of the team.

After what seemed an age, the umpire's finger went up. Tendulkar was out, leg before wicket, bowled Panesar.

Monty leapt up and down, punched the air with his fist and yelled with delight.

It was his first Test wicket. There would be many more, but this one – his first – would always be special.

It was, after all, the wicket of his hero Tendulkar, who had signed his bat for him all those years ago at Luton.

Fact file
Monty Panesar

✦ Full name: Mudhsuden Singh Panesar

✦ Born: Luton, Bedfordshire
25th April 1982

1994	Plays for Bedfordshire Under 13's
1998	Youngest ever player to be selected for Bedfordshire 1st XI
2001	County debut for Northants. England Under 19's debut. Wins the Denis Compton Award 2001
2005	Graduates from Loughborough University and becomes full member of Northants team, taking 46 wickets at an average of 21.54 runs
2006	Selected by England to tour India. Takes three wickets in his first match, including that of his hero, Sachin Tendulkar
2006	Plays for England against Sri Lanka and Pakistan. Takes eight wickets in the second test
2007	Gets his first ten wicket Test haul in the third Test against the West Indies. Named England's 'Man of the Series'. Named 'Wisden Cricketer of the Year'
2008	Best ever Test figures of 6–37 – against New Zealand

Hope Powell

The boy was new to the area and wanted to show that he was the best football player around. He swerved round a small kid from the opposition. Then he ran on, but the ball was no longer at his feet. That little kid must've taken the ball off him without him knowing it!

The boy turned round. The small kid thumped the ball past the goalkeeper at the other end of the road. The opposition erupted into cheers.

A couple of other players on his side were shaking their heads in disbelief. "Who is that kid?" he asked them.

"That's my sister," said one of them, with a sigh.

"Her name's Hope Powell," added his friend. "And she's the best player on the street."

**Continue reading this story in
DREAM TO WIN: Hope Powell**

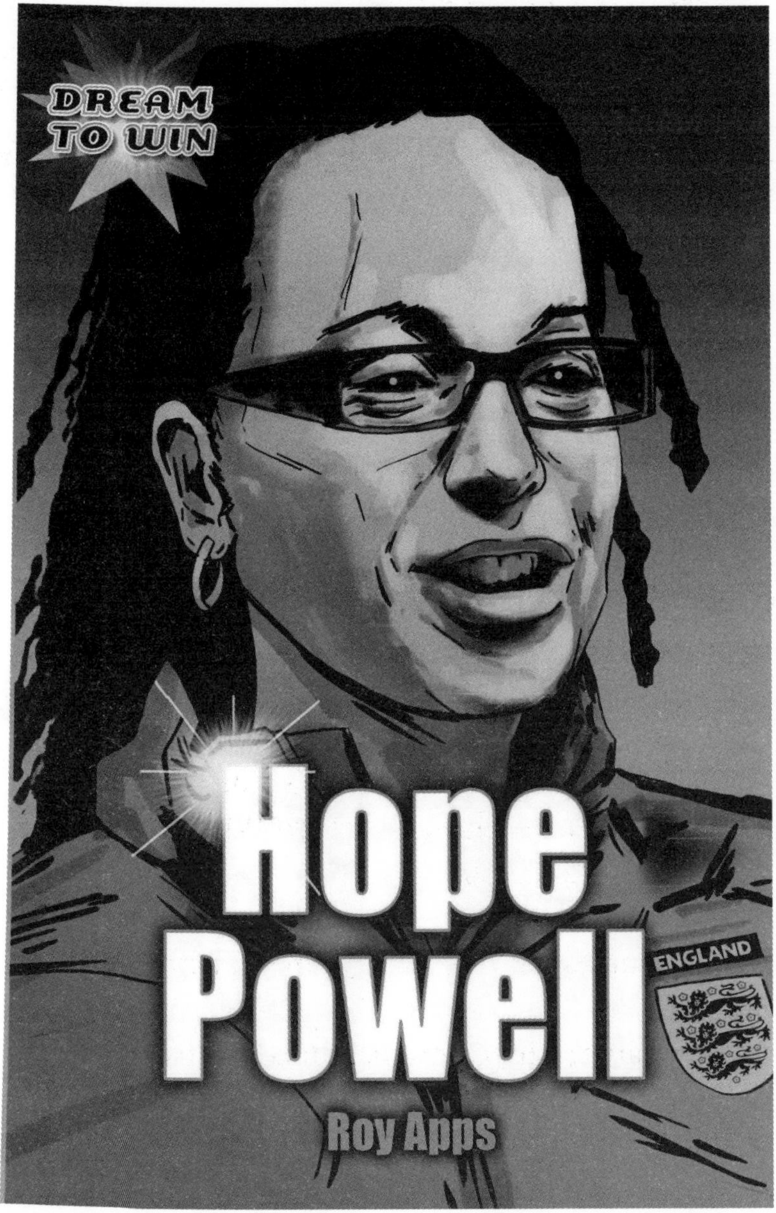
DREAM TO WIN
Hope Powell
ENGLAND
Roy Apps

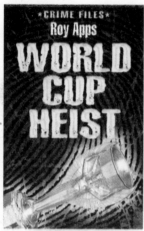

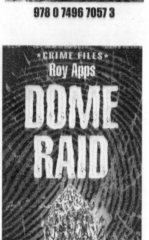